R   n Liverpool, in 1945, V
f   priesthood in Rome. He v   ⌐⌐ ⌐⌐ ⌐⌐ for
t   chdiocese of Liverpool and then served parishes in
\   and Toxteth. In 1992, he became an auxiliary bishop
t   stminster and then Archbishop of Birmingham in
;   In 2009, he was installed as the eleventh Archbishop
(estminster and hosted Pope Benedict during the
]   l Visit to the UK in 2010. On 22 February 2014, he
v   created Cardinal by Pope Francis. In addition to being
]   on of a number of Catholic charities, including the
H   ge and the Cardinal Hume Centre, he is also the first
     cellor of St Mary's University, Twickenham. Recently,
     unched the Santa Marta Group to combat human
     cking and opened Bakhita House in London, a ref-
     or survivors of human trafficking. Cardinal Nichols
     knowledged as a strong campaigner for the vulner-
     in society and a leading advocate for interfaith co-
o   ation and integration. He is also a keen, lifelong fan
(verpool Football Club.

HOPE IN ACTION

Reaching out to a world in need

Vincent Nichols

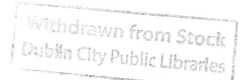

First published in Great Britain in 2017

Society for Promoting Christian Knowledge
36 Causton Street
London SW1P 4ST
www.spck.org.uk

British Library Cataloguing-in-Publication Data
A catalogue record for this book is available from the British Library

ISBN 978–0–281–07836–3
eBook ISBN 978–0–281–07837–0

1 3 5 7 9 10 8 6 4 2

Typeset by Manila Typesetting Company
Manufacture managed by Jellyfish
Printed in Great Britain by CPI

eBook by Manila Typesetting Company

Produced on paper from sustainable forests

To Henry Joseph and Mary,
the first and best of teachers.

Contents

Foreword

What makes us human? Cardinal Nichols' question, at the end of this wonderful collection of reflections, is the question of our time. What holds us together across cultures, religions, gender and many other differences, and how do we live together in ways that honour the image of God within each and every human being?

Cardinal Nichols' answers are both deeply realistic, and deeply hopeful. He names some of the great evils of our time – the dehumanization of others through slavery and sexual exploitation, through radicalization, through poverty and marginalization – and names the root of them all, unflinchingly: the tendency of the human heart to dismiss the other, to turn aside from the one who suffers, to seek its own benefit at the expense of others. Yet he does not dwell upon the problem, but, with profound compassion and humanity, consistently draws our eyes towards another reality. He ceaselessly reminds us of the work of the Spirit around us, in every person, and calls us to recognize and join in the mission of God, to proclaim God's love and power in word and action. He does not offer grand solutions or unworkable schemes but points to the difference that every person can make if they open themselves to God and choose to see those around them as made in his image, however distorted that image may be.

Hence this is a book of hope, as the title suggests. A book about practical hope, hope for every day, everywhere and every person. It is about recognizing and nurturing signs of hope around us. It is about the hope that faithfulness in the small things of life can make a difference that reaches far beyond what we can imagine; hope that rests on God's incommensurable love for human beings and the power of his Spirit at work within and without us. And it is a hope that propels us to action, not out of guilt or duty, but rooted in seeing the world and its people through the eyes of God and joining God at work in that world. It is hope rooted in prayer, worked out in reconciliation that reaches out to others with love, healing and the good news of Jesus Christ.

Justin Welby
Archbishop of Canterbury

Preface

This book arises from a series of talks and lectures I gave, many of them during the Year of Mercy (8 December 2015 to 20 November 2016) declared by Pope Francis. I first of all look at what we mean by Christian hope, and what it means to be a disciple with a mission, before looking at the importance of mercy and some particular situations in which God asks us to put our Christian hope into action.

My hope is that this book, and the questions at the end of each chapter, will encourage you to be strong in your faith and in the works of mercy that spring from it.

1

Rumours of hope

There are many places in the world today where hope is in short supply. One is Erbil, among the many thousands of Christian refugees who have fled from the plain of Nineveh. Another is Gaza, where over one million Muslims are held. There can be a shortage of hope in some of our own prisons or even on some of our own streets. The concept of hope was very much on my mind after visiting Yad Vashem, the Holocaust Memorial in Jerusalem, in 2014. This Memorial poses questions about hope in the most radical manner possible.

Yad Vashem is a powerful tribute to all who perished in the Holocaust and a damning indictment of all who perpetrated it, directly or indirectly. On my visit, only slowly did these perceptions sink deeply into my consciousness.

The journey through Yad Vashem is long and needs time. I went without a guide, with a small group of people. Fairly quickly on its zig-zag paths I lost touch with my companions. In fact I lost touch with everything: time, space, wider purpose. I quickly became absorbed in the horrendous history that was claiming my undivided attention. As I walked its paths, I had a sense of being drawn into a closed world, or rather into an understanding of how the world systematically closed its doors to the Jewish people, leaving them to their dreadful fate. Never before had I understood how abandoned they were, left without any place to go, or to call their own.

Then, too, I was drawn into the personal horrors of the victims of the Holocaust, told and retold, city by city, family by family, until reduced to yet another corpse brutally bulldozed into a pit. Never before had I felt in my deepest being the impact of the total degradation of the human person, executed on an industrial scale and here presented before my eyes.

The questions flooded in, both at the time and afterwards. How could this have happened? What are the roots of this evil? What are its consequences for generation after generation of those who perished and of those who survived? How do we live with this aspect of our past, the presence of evil in our midst?

Sin is a reality. No one remains untouched by it. But does not this Holocaust of sin and evil demand that we stop any talk of human goodness and simply stay silent in front of its abyss in which surely all hope is lost?

Yet even in Yad Vashem traces of enduring goodness are to be found. They emerge in the indomitable endurance shown by so many in the Nazi killing camps. The last words spoken by many in the gas chambers were: 'Next year, Jerusalem.' Traces of heroic goodness are found in the lives of those who risked all to shelter Jewish people and form with them the powerful bond, that alliance of secrecy, between the hunted and the protector. Sometimes, in Yad Vashem, I had to read the small print to find these stories. But they are there. And today this same heroism is recognized in granting the title 'Righteous Gentile' to those whose stories of astonishing courage emerge only now.

Perhaps there are indeed moments in which the small print of the messages of hope seemingly disappears from sight. There are many when it does not. Ours is surely the task of keeping alive these rumours of hope, however we understand them, and of knitting them together so that the far horizons of an eternal hope may never be lost to our sight.

The Holocaust may not be the most obvious starting point for thinking about hope, but it actually poses the questions very sharply: What do we mean by hope? Where, if anywhere, can we find hope? How do we understand that hope? How and where is it generated? What is its deepest nature?

What is hope?

Hope is not the same as optimism. Optimism is a disposition 'to whistle a merry tune', 'to look on the bright side', however irrational, whatever the state of things. It may or may not be realistic.

Hope is something else. The great philosopher and theologian St Thomas Aquinas treats hope in two distinct, but intimately related, parts. He first presents hope as a natural passion arising from a desire for something that is understood to be good, though it is not yet possessed; difficult, but not impossible, to attain. Hope is a movement of the will, a striving towards such a future good: an appetite which stirs up confidence and grants assurance. Thus hope abounds in young people and drunkards!

> *A hope-filled person is spurred into action when faced with something desirable, yet hard to achieve*

More seriously, hope moves us to become pilgrims. A hope-filled person is spurred into action when faced with something desirable, yet hard to achieve. Such hope is not the product of opinion or argument alone. We do not acquire hope just by having a point of view. There has to be something else – an impetus to act, a vision, something from within our understanding that fires our imagination, a drive consciously exercised in the effort to achieve a possible yet still a future good. Hope is a partnership between *both* our understanding and our will. It moves us to get something done, something demanding, something that will make a difference. Hope gets you out of bed. Lack of hope leaves you reaching for the duvet.

Where can we find hope?

Understood this way, our world is full of signs of hope. They surround us every day. They come as daily strivings to establish, maintain, express or consolidate efforts to attain something both desired and difficult to achieve. No matter how broken our world, no matter how lacking in overall vision, there are countless fragments of hope.

What kinds of fragments do I mean? They are often the experiences of our daily lives to which we respond with warmth of heart, a quiet smile of gratitude and admiration: a neighbour's kindness, a friend's compassion, the utter generosity of a lover, the creativeness of a gifted person brought to a good purpose, be it the generation of wealth or a work of charity. These stories do not fill our newspapers; but they do fill our hearts and encourage us along the way.

These fragments express the strivings of hope and are themselves generative of hope in others. We can see well enough how each of them is a tiny masterpiece designed to strengthen a hope that something difficult will be achieved: the relief of suffering, the faithfulness of love, the ending of poverty, the creation of new jobs or new wealth.

More challenging is to see how these tiny fragments are in fact pieces of a mosaic, the 'tesserae' which when brought together can make a fine and inspiring work of art. I believe that this challenge is made all the more difficult, at least in part, by the culture of cynicism in which we live. This culture urges us to view with suspicion reports or even experiences of goodness. It tutors us to attribute to others the worst of motives, or at least to seriously entertain that perspective. World-weariness teaches us to be cautious. The misdemeanours of many institutions, including my own, emphasize that lesson. Nevertheless, we may have to learn afresh to see what is actually before us: the innate goodness of so many people.

Another factor making the formation of a coherent view of hope problematic is our culture's embrace of relativism. By the logic of relativism nothing that others do in pursuit of their hopes or ideals is necessarily related to me since notions of what is truly good (and truly evil) are privatized. That may be good for her, but is of no interest or relevance to me. To nurture and benefit from the generative capacities of the hope we see around us, we may have to give more attention to those fragments which, if brought together, have the capacity to defeat both cynicism and relativism.

The generative capacities of hope

Let me reflect briefly on three aspects of our relationships which seem to me particularly important in thinking about how we assemble a larger picture, of which we are all a part, and thereby strengthen the generative capacities for hope. I use the word 'generative' because the capacity for hope is something which, given the right conditions, can grow and flourish in individuals and in society.

First, the family: our initial school of life and love. We know much about the conditions needed for the life-giving bonding of infants to their parents. Evidence for the lifelong consequences of early childhood trauma and dislocation is powerful. The experience of healthy childhood development, including experiencing failure and forgiveness, and the learning of gratitude, deeply influences our adult selves and our capacity for hope and trust in others. It follows that a society that cares about the quality of hope for the future will care hugely, in an objective and systematic way, about factors which help or hinder the family.

Second, beyond but founded on the family, is what Rabbi Jonathan Sachs speaks of as the social sphere. He describes this sphere as 'covenantal', always based on a kind of covenant we make with others as we engage together in work or projects, outside of the political or economic spheres. This covenantal activity generates trust between us. Effective political life and creative economic activity depend on trust. But they do not so easily generate trust. In fact they tend to consume trust. So the social sphere is crucial: it is the place where our identity as social beings, whose fulfilment is bound up with that of others, finds expression. But more importantly in this place, hope is something carried by the community and not just by the individual. For a common project or goal that is difficult yet possible to attain, one week your commitment and belief stirs me from my apathy and despondency; but the next week I may be full of hope and cheer you along.

Third, the imagination. The capacity of art to stimulate hope should not be underestimated. A friend told me a story of a group coming together in a poor area of Bristol to hear about deep-seated social problems and the acute difficulties of effecting real change. Halfway through the meeting there was a performance by a local choir, its members aged from 10 to 80 years. The effect was dramatic. When the meeting resumed, the mood was wholly different. The choir's imagination kindled in the group hope for what might be and invigorated them to act.

These are some of the ways in which we can bring together isolated fragments of hope into a wider and more coherent picture, thereby strengthening their generative capacity. The more we construct and contemplate that picture, the more we are encouraged to seize some of the difficult things we know are for our good and believe that they are achievable.

But we have to go further. Indeed, I suggest that both our experience and reasoning requires us to do so. Take the experience of being moved by a piece of art or music. We are taken out of ourselves. We move beyond the moment into something timeless. We reach for another horizon, an instinctively emerging sense of cohesion about all things, or conversely, the challenge of radical meaninglessness. The invitation is clear: radical hope or despair.

Hopeful pilgrims

This leads us back to St Thomas and part two of his consideration of hope. Here he brings into focus the ultimate good towards which hope compels us: the mystery of

Hope directs us towards God, the source and summit of all good

God. Hope has as its ultimate object our radical happiness. That happiness comes with our presence before and within God. Hope directs us towards God, the source and summit of all good: Goodness itself. Realizing this enables us to recognize that among all that God gives us are the means by which we may attain this perfect happiness. So for Thomas the full description of hope reads: 'Wherefore, in so far as we hope for anything as being possible to us by means of Divine assistance, our hope attains to God Himself, on Whose help it leans.'[1]

This is what makes us truly pilgrims. Over and over again we grasp that we are 'not yet' there, still to achieve our true and deepest purpose. In the language of faith, this is the simple recognition of our creatureliness, the fundamental fact of the inner structure of our lives. Put it this way: if we are not creatures, beings loved into existence by a creator who acts with intentions, then our journey is towards nothingness and our present entirely without lasting meaning. God's grace infuses our natural hope – our stretching forth with restless hearts for the future good, difficult but possible to attain – with the imprint of its true purpose, one that is at the same time intensely fulfilling yet truly daunting. Our home lies beyond us. Yet our hearts and our reason reach out towards that home, and the gift of God makes it truly attainable.

Our reason for hope is the never-ending mercy of God, who pours out his life that we might see and live again

Such hope is at the core of contemporary Christian humanism. It drives Pope Francis to embrace the profoundly disfigured man, to kiss the feet of the Muslim girl, to harangue the ideology of global capitalism for its disdain for people, especially the poor, to proclaim ceaselessly that our reason for hope is the never-ending mercy of God, who pours out his life that we might see and live again.

For reflection or discussion

1 Can you think of a time when you felt particularly hopeful? How did that feeling of hope inspire you to behave differently?

2 What does it mean to feel 'hopeless'? Are there people you know who feel hopeless? What can you do to generate some hope in their lives?

3 What are the signs of hope in your family, your community, your parish? How might you build on these?

4 What can you do to bring hope to others in your local community and in the wider world?

2

Missionary disciples

When I celebrated my seventieth birthday in 2015 I was hit with the realization that, God willing, I only had another five years left of being Archbishop of Westminster. I was filled with a new sense of urgency: the years are passing so quickly and there is simply so much to do, particularly when it comes to sharing the great message of our faith.

How well is the Church measuring up to Jesus' command in Matthew 28.19 to 'Go, therefore, make disciples of all the nations; baptise them in the name of the Father and of the Son and of the Holy Spirit, and teach them to observe all the commands I gave you'?

In December 1962 this question was posed as a plan for the entire Second Vatican Council under Pope John XXIII. It was followed by this remark: 'In order to respond to the Saviour's command the whole Church must be put on a missionary footing!' Decades later, and now inspired by Pope Francis, we are still determined that this shall be so. Indeed, Pope Francis' favourite description for us is 'missionary disciples': disciples because we are focused on Christ, missionary because we are sharing his mission to the world.[1]

The task of every Christian is to spread the Good News, to share with others, in word and deed, a relationship with Christ so that they are prompted to discover Jesus for themselves.

The great commission

Jesus issues the command to 'Go, therefore, make disciples of all the nations' right at the end of his ministry, but not because it is some sort of afterthought. Rather, he has saved this command for the last, crucial moments in which he gives us our marching orders. This command is the central purpose of his incarnation, of his life, of his death, of his resurrection, and of his return to the Father. His final prayer, addressed to his heavenly Father, is: 'As you have sent me into the world, I have sent them into the world' (John 17.18).

This is our mandate, our mission, and it is central to our identity. By baptism we are made one with Christ. What is his is to be ours. His mission is ours. He was 'sent by the Father' so that the world 'may have life and have it to the full' and this charge is handed on to us.

This mission, given to Jesus by the Father, flows through all eternity, for he is the eternal Word, through whom that gift of life is first given. And he becomes the incarnate Word, so that the gift of life may reach its fulfilment. This is the mission of the Father's heart: the outflow of his creative love, now flowing to us, in our need, as the eternal mercy of the Father.

This is the work of the Holy Spirit, the energy of the Father and Son, their love, their fire, their creativity, moving and moulding us. In his final prayer, Jesus refers everything to the Holy Spirit. The Spirit will teach and guide us; the Spirit will come only if he goes; through the Holy Spirit mercy will spring into the action of the forgiveness of our sins.

To understand our mission we have to go to the heart of God

To understand our mission we have to go to the heart of God, the very mystery of the Holy Trinity, the inner life of God. This is spoken of as the divine *communion*: the sharing within the mystery of the persons of God of divine life, love, truth, goodness and beauty. Only from within that inner heart of God does our mission arise. Only from that inner heart of God does our mission find its shape, its purpose, its energy. We are to do something beautiful, something that is of God, something that is for God.

So, our mission always starts in our prayer, flows from prayer, from our daily openness to the great mystery of the life of God. It cannot start anywhere else.

The Church as communio

Since the Second Vatican Council we have talked of the Church, or the parish, as a *communio*: a communion

14

or even as a community. But this has little depth unless the word *communio* refers first of all to the life of God. The Church is a *communio* in and through the communion of life of the Father, Son and Holy Spirit. Only because we have been drawn, together, into that life are we a community. We are not a group of like-minded people who agree a programme of action. We are participants together in the mystery of God. Everything about our Church flows from there. Everything about our parish flows from there – at least everything worth having!

Parishes are not really communities unless they are rooted in the *communio* of the life of God. Nothing else will hold us together. Our striving after that sharing of life, of love, of truth, of goodness, of beauty which flows from God is the only thing that makes sense of parish life. That is why the celebration of Mass is our central act; why we say that the Eucharist makes the Church. This is why our life of prayer is essential; why our pondering of the Scriptures is crucial; why our gazing on our Lord present in the Blessed Sacrament is our silent centre.

The *communio* of the parish flows from the *communio* of God. The mission of the parish flows from the mission of God: the sending forth of the Son, by the Father, in the power of the Holy Spirit. This 'mystery of our salvation' gives shape to our life, to our prayer and to all of our work. 'As you, Father, have sent me into the world, so I am sending them into the world' (John 17.18).

How is it that we are members of the Church? Because Jesus has called us, in a thousand different ways. And we can go back one step further. It is the Father's will that Jesus calls each one of us. Each of us is a gift given by the Father to his Son to be his companions, to share in his mission. We are here because it is the will of the Father to send us into the world!

Think of the calling of the first 12 disciples, the Apostles. No one forced them to follow. They were invited. They were called to be with Jesus. That was the first step: called into a communion of life with him, into a 'divine *communio*'.

The disciples were so different from each other. Matthew was a tax collector, hated by most people as a traitor, a collaborator with the oppressive Roman authorities. Simon was a Zealot, committed to the liberation of his people. They were called together by Jesus. In any other circumstance, Simon would have knifed Matthew, killing him on the spot. In the *communio* of Jesus something else is at work, something which is far greater than human commitment, or a human cause.

If we are to be missionary disciples we too must become part of this community. We have to enter deeply into the life of our Lord, as flowing from the Father, and be sustained and empowered by the Holy Spirit.

The Holy Spirit and mission

There are two ways in which we should understand the action of the Holy Spirit as central to our mission.

The first is that the Holy Spirit precedes us wherever we may go, or be sent. I remember going one evening to the Financial Standards Board in the City of London to take part in a dinner discussion about ethics in banking. I felt very out of my depth! But I was consoled by the fact that the Holy Spirit was already there: in the goodness of the people I met, in their deep unease at what was happening in their profession, in their puzzling over what was to be done. Don't go into any situation believing it is godless. A very experienced and well-established defence counsel said to me that among all the murderers, cheats and villains he had defended he had never met a person who was all evil. The Holy Spirit is always there before us! If we miss that presence we will lose our way!

The second thing we have to remember in our mission is that the Holy Spirit will give us the gifts we need. The Holy Spirit will give us that discernment of what to do, of what to say, of how to bring faith to life in this particular moment. The Holy Spirit gives us this *sensus fidei*, this 'feel' for faith in action.[2] Jesus told

> *The Holy Spirit will give us that discernment of what to do, of what to say, of how to bring faith to life*

his disciples not to be too bothered about preparing every detail of what they were going to say. Evangelization is not about superior planning, greater efficiency and high-class management. It is about love and trust and openness to the Holy Spirit.

A splendid example of what I mean is a movement called Mother's Prayers. It was started in England in 1995 by two women who felt led by the Lord to pray together for their children and grandchildren. There are now thousands of groups of Christian mothers – from all denominations, in over 100 countries – who meet and pray together for their children.

Here are some of their axioms:

'We must always let God be God: keep it simple, let God bless you and make you holy.'

'In Mother's Prayers we can take our masks off. God called us to be here. We've all said "Yes". Nothing is too difficult for God.'

'"Lord, I can't but you can", that's what Mother's Prayers is. Give each day to the Lord, and opportunities will come.'

'Always ask for gentleness and a loving approach.'[3]

The movement spread entirely without deliberation, just by the power of example and providence. It brings to the Lord mothers who live in the most difficult circumstances:

a Russian mother who has had six abortions, a South American mother whose children are drug addicts and drug dealers, an African mother whose children are victims of human trafficking. In small groups, mothers pray, they place their children before the Lord and they find his peace. And it has all been led simply by the Holy Spirit.

To whom are we sent?

We know that we are sent 'to the world', but this is a rather large task and it can be hard to know where to begin. It may help to think of 'the world' in more specific categories, or in terms of the three Cs.

First, we are sent to our *colleagues* who have lost their way. These can be fellow Christians who are resting: all those who cross the threshold of the church just every now and then. They have heard of Jesus; they have some of the words; they have a familiarity, of sorts, with the Church.

Can we lead them, step by step, to know Jesus more clearly? It's a bit like the first proclamations of Peter. He wanted to move his hearers from a first familiarity, as Jews, with the person of Jesus and open for them a true knowledge and subsequent love for him. There are countless opportunities to explore: for instance, how can the 300 regular worshippers in a parish reach out to the 1,500 who cross the threshold in the course of a year, or who might do so if invited?

Second, we are sent to the *curious*. A few years ago I overheard a conversation in a Spanish church. Two willowy, blond youngsters said to their mother: 'Who's that naked man up there on a cross?' They were keen to know more. Or, I was asked some time ago why there were so many cars parked up outside the church every Sunday morning: 'Is it a car-boot sale?'

Curiosity, even if tinged with hostility, can be a marvellous opportunity if we are open to it and remember that within that curiosity may well lie the prompting of the Holy Spirit. If we forget that, then we are quickly on the defensive and the moment has gone!

Curiosity often arises out of a sense of wanting something more, a sense of emptiness. This is how some feel today, unsure about the deeper meaning of their lives, about what they stand for, beyond their loved ones or their possessions. Curiosity can actually save the cat!

We know that Jesus answers those deepest longings. He is the fullness of truth about who we truly are. The pathway of the beatitudes (Matthew 5.3–12) is the pathway of human fulfilment. There is an answer for the curious!

Third, and probably the most important group of all, we are sent to those who *cry from the heart*, from confusion, pain, hunger, loneliness, need and anger.

When Jesus sent us out into the world, he was, at that moment, experiencing in his flesh the worst of the world:

its intrigues, its betrayals and, shortly, its capacity for inflicting pain even unto death. But he did not turn away. The cry of his prayer mingled with the cry of the world and redeemed it.

So too for us. Whatever action we take in response to the cry of the world around us must bring together the cry of prayer and the cry of pain. Only then can it be the mission of Jesus.

Of course our action should be effective. But even more so it should be prayerful; otherwise its effectiveness will not touch the deepest well of pain from which the cry is rising. For, in the words of Pope Francis, 'The joy of the gospel fills the hearts and lives of all who encounter Jesus. Those who accept his offer of salvation are set free from sin, sorrow, inner emptiness and loneliness.'[4]

Pope Francis has since added to these words encouragement that our mission is always about bringing back together all that is broken, working for the deepest unity. He said:

> It would be facile to think that division and hatred only concerns struggles between countries or groups in society. Rather, they are a manifestation of the 'widespread individualism' which divides us and sets us against one another (*Evangelii Gaudium*, 99), that legacy of sin lurking in the heart of human beings which causes so much suffering in society and all of creation. But it is precisely

this troubled world into which Jesus sends us. We must not respond with nonchalance, or complain we do not have the resources to do the job, or that the problems are too big. Instead, we must respond by taking up the cry of Jesus and accepting the grace and challenge of being builders of unity.[5]

Now is the time

Ensuring that our parishes become missionary parishes, communities of evangelization, rooted in the mystery of God and sharing in the mission of Jesus himself, is a long process. But I feel that we are at a crucial moment. It seems as though a fairly long winter is slowly beginning to thaw, a winter in which there was great opposition to the things of faith and in which we had to learn to face our failings with proper penitence and humility. But now I sense something of an opportunity. I sense a more evident uncertainty in our society about how we should go about things, a troubled sense that all is far from well: the sharp and widening divisions between rich and poor; the troubled world around us that casts millions of people as refugees, some of whom are just outside, knocking on our door. How are we to react?

We must become evangelizing parishes; parishes that are centred on the Lord, always in prayer, always seeking his face and always following his calling into the world. As individuals and as a church we can begin by looking at the rich gifts we have been given and asking how we might use them to proclaim the mercy of God to the world.

For reflection or discussion

1 How can your parish foster a sense of *communio*?
2 How might you and your parish bring Good News to the group identified as 'colleagues', that is, fellow Christians who have lost their way or are resting?
3 How might you and your parish reach out to the group identified as those who are 'curious' about faith?
4 How might you become a 'missionary disciple'?

3

Agents of mercy

At the end of the last chapter I identified the third, and probably most important, group to whom we are commanded to bring the Good News of Jesus: those who cry from the heart, from confusion, pain, hunger, loneliness, need and anger.

I believe that the unbounded mercy of God is the starting point, the lens through which we can look, as we seek to proclaim the gospel in a world that cries out for the hope it offers.

Understanding God's mercy

Jesus is the face of God's mercy. In him the love, compassion and forgiveness of God takes its fullest human expression

Jesus is the face of God's mercy. In him the love, compassion and forgiveness of God takes its fullest human expression. To look at Jesus is to see how the Eternal Father looks on us. In the face of Jesus we see that our Father is prepared to do anything, everything, to draw us to the love for which we have been made. God's mercy is the shape taken by the love of God when it comes face to face with our broken human reality. God weeps and pours out his heart in Jesus that we may know how much he longs for us to be with him for ever.

Jesus is the face of God's mercy. But we are to be the hands, voices and actions of that mercy in the flesh of our world today. Here we must remember again that everything we have to do and say in the name of Jesus springs not from ideas, nor from study, but from our relationship with him. God's mercy is not an idea. It is a reality, the fullness of love offered to us in Jesus. In other words, the only way in which we truly learn about this mercy is by experiencing it in our own lives. If mercy is to be the hallmark of all we do, it must first be the hallmark of our relationship with our blessed Lord. And this comes about when, in the deepest part of our being, we know that we stand in need of that mercy for we acknowledge that we too are broken and marked by sin. When we have received his mercy, when we have been caressed by mercy, then it flows from within our hearts and we are ready to offer it to others and find in that mercy the source of all that we do.

One way of understanding the depth of God's mercy is to start at the very beginning. The first act of God's mercy is the act of creation. God's Spirit hovers over the 'darkness' and an ordered universe emerges. Thus we live in a 'cosmos', an ordered world, and not in chaos. The ordering of creation is to its fulfilment and not to its ultimate annihilation. This is a great mercy, an enormous blessing.

Similarly, we can say that the second great act of God's mercy is that God calls each person into existence with a destiny, a purpose, a 'design' for every one of us. God's purpose for every single human being is that we come to share in God's eternal life. We are not called into being just to live an 'existential moment' and then be extinguished. We are not created for futility. We are given the gift of life for this great destiny: to dwell with God in fulfilment and joy for ever!

God's loving mercy not only gives us this vision of our world and of ourselves; it also makes this vision possible to achieve. In Jesus, the fullest manifestation of the Father's loving design, all is made possible. Through Christ, all of creation will come through its time of great groaning and be raised to its fulfilment (Romans 8.18–26). In union with Christ through baptism we will be brought into the very heart of the life of the Blessed Trinity. And in the power of the Holy Spirit we can live each day not only in hope and anticipation of that joy but also, in our daily efforts, serving its realization, its heralding.

What are the works of mercy?

What does it mean to bring about this realization, this heralding, in practice? It means that we should carry out the works of mercy, both spiritual and corporal.

The Spiritual Works of Mercy are to: admonish the sinner; instruct the ignorant; counsel the doubtful; comfort the sorrowful; bear wrongs patiently; forgive all injuries; pray for the living and the dead. These are the responses of loving faith to the needs of the heart and soul deep within every human being.

God has created each person to dwell in the glory of God's presence for ever. This is the ultimate vocation of every human being. The spiritual works of mercy serve the fulfilment of that purpose. To offer counsel to the lost and confused

The spiritual works of mercy are all the nudges and encouragement we give each other on our pilgrimage to God

is to help them redirect their lives to their true purpose. So also to instruct the ignorant, to admonish those who are heading in an erroneous direction, to comfort the lost and bereaved, to forgive those who have offended us, to be patient with those who truly test us and always to pray for the living and the dead is precisely to serve the great mercy of God who has created us for such a high destiny. The spiritual works of mercy are all the nudges and encouragement we give each other on our pilgrimage to God.

The Corporal Works of Mercy are to: feed the hungry; give drink to the thirsty; clothe the naked; shelter the homeless; visit the sick; visit the imprisoned and bury the dead. These are the responses of loving faith to the physical needs which cause many to cry out.

God has created for us an ordered world in which to live. Yet it is not always experienced or seen to be so. The corporal works of mercy are the practical ways in which, day by day, we re-establish and regenerate the mercy of God's ordered creation. When we give food to the hungry, give drink to the thirsty, clothe the naked, welcome the stranger, heal the sick, visit the imprisoned and bury the dead we are restoring a proper sense of order. No one should be left thirsty, naked, lost in sickness, isolated in jail, unwelcomed in their need, left abandoned and unburied in death. When those things happen, as they do every day and on a great scale, any sense that we are living in an ordered world is rendered implausible.

The corporal works of mercy, then, are the ways in which in my neighbourhood, on my street, in my community, I can help to restore that sense of place and belonging, of respect and acceptance that our cosmic home, as created by God, should embody.

Mercy in practice

The practice of the corporal and spiritual works of mercy gives a human face to the presence of divine mercy. Let me take one of the corporal acts of mercy as an example: to shelter the homeless.

A walk through the streets of any city at night, or early morning, will soon make clear the extent of the problem of homelessness in our society. According to Crisis, the national charity for homelessness, there have been sustained increases in people who are homeless, or threatened by homelessness, over the last six years.[1] Charities have felt greater strain as local authorities have cut back on homelessness prevention and on Supporting People budgets. We are also witnessing a rise in hidden homelessness, people who are under the radar of the official statistics. For example, people who may have lost their job and who are sleeping on sofas, or in spare rooms or in bed and breakfasts because they do not have a home of their own; or young people who stay with a different friend each night or go to all-night parties to avoid sleeping on the streets.[2]

Once someone has lost their home it is extremely difficult for them to find work, claim benefit or find somewhere to rent; the person soon becomes caught in what Crisis calls the 'homelessness trap'. So preventing homelessness in the first place must be a priority. Of course, every homeless person has a unique story to tell, but the contributing factors to homelessness are often similar. Family relationship breakdown is a leading contributor to homelessness among single men, and a leading cause of family breakdown is financial difficulty. Then there is the scourge of drug and alcohol addiction. And, of course, those without suitable accommodation upon release from prison are the most likely to find themselves on the streets, back in a vicious cycle that will often result in them returning to prison.

Charities respond with dynamism and creativity to these challenges. Marriage Care works hard to support family relationships. This year Depaul UK worked with more than 1,400 offenders through prison-based advocacy services. Members of the Catholic network are working to support people who have fallen into addiction. Housing Justice has a network of winter night shelters across England and Wales. Each night more than 1,000 homeless people will find a welcome in over 50 churches across England. Caritas Salford's Cornerstone Centre, among many others, provides support for 150 regular visitors who come for a hot meal, a shower, a haircut, a community nurse and access to the internet for accommodation and job searches, and provides advice and emergency accommodation for 50 people every day. For every paid member of staff, they have an impressive ten volunteers! All over England and Wales, parishes and charities offer a range of support to people who are homeless: from extensive skills training, counselling, hostels and move-on accommodation, to simply offering a hot meal and clothing to those with nowhere else to turn. Indeed, in the Diocese of Westminster we calculate that in our parishes over 4 million hours of volunteers' time is given every year.

This is mercy, love and hope in action: sharing the goods of one of the wealthiest societies on earth with those at its peripheries, with the victims of economic and social systems that remain heartless unless enlivened by a sense of moral purpose and generosity.

This work is rooted in faith in God, in God who gives each person an innate dignity that is to be upheld no matter the circumstances, and in God who gives his grace, in a thousand different ways, to raise our fallen nature to this steady and determined desire to create here a better society, one which reflects more closely God's compassion and mercy, which we all so clearly need.

Mercy and evangelization

Any one of these works of mercy is an opportunity to share the Good News. That work is never forgotten by the recipient and often leads that person on the pathway to Christ, to him who inspired the loving generosity in the first place.

Every work of evangelization can also be related to these works of mercy and, if they are rightly conceived and carried out, clearly display that mercy to all involved. Thus, our efforts will serve to proclaim again that God's work of creation is purposeful, that God's call to every person is the deepest meaning of our life, the foundation of our dignity. The restoration of these horizons, step by step through our actions, is a true proclamation of the gospel and a clear invitation to know Christ Jesus more clearly and to follow him more nearly, for he alone is the vision of this truth and he alone is the one in whom it is attainable.

As Pope Francis knows, every person, whether we think of ourselves as religious or not, longs for the embrace of mercy, the love that accepts us as we are and, at the same time, calls us to become what we are made to be. Or, as Pope St John Paul II said, 'Apart from the mercy of God, there is no other source of hope for mankind!'[3]

I am reminded of that wonderful moment at the end of the Gospel of St Luke, when two of the disciples are on the road to Emmaus. For them the realization that Jesus was risen from the dead changed everything. Now they knew him! Now they were truly in a hurry to let others know this great truth, for they were truly embraced by the mercy of Jesus, coming to them in their dismay and solitude and turning their sadness into joy. As Sandra Schneiders writes:

> Inflamed with his Spirit they rush back to Jerusalem to share with the rest of the Church what they now know from their own experience: Jesus is alive. And they hear from the others the echo of their own experience, that He has appeared also to Simon, and to others. And over the days, and down through the centuries, the stories keep coming in. I saw Him. He spoke to me. He is with us. He is not dead. Death has no hold over Him nor, because of Him, over us. Jesus is alive! Alleluia![4]

This is the witness we too are to give in our day. We too hear these same stories and we too tell them ourselves, in word and deed. He is alive. He is not dead. We know him. We hear his voice. He is with us always!

For reflection or discussion

1 When did you last carry out one of the spiritual works of mercy? How might you ensure that their practice becomes a part of your daily life?
2 How can your hands, voice and actions bring God's mercy to the world?
3 How might you and your parish bring God's mercy to those who 'cry from the heart'?
4 Choose one of the corporal works of mercy and decide what you could do for the next six months to show God's mercy to those people. You could consider volunteering for a charity.

4

Ending sexual violence and abuse

In our efforts to improve the lives of the most needy and vulnerable in our societies we often rightly speak of wanting to protect human rights. In order for this language of human rights to be robust, we need to be clear about its foundations.

The entry of human rights into the international legal framework is largely welcomed. But human rights themselves do not derive from a legal system or from a political authority or from a state. The dignity of every person, and the pattern of rights which flow from that dignity, are inherent in the person herself or himself. They are inalienable. So what exactly is the foundation of human rights?

The dignity of every person arises from within their nature and that nature is most clearly understood as deriving from its Creator, from the mystery of God

The dignity of every person arises from within their nature and that nature is most clearly understood as deriving from its Creator, from the mystery of God. This is an important contribution of religious faith. It sharpens our rational understanding and deepens our sense of who we are and the dignity which is properly ours. Within this God-given dignity, the right to life itself and the right to bodily integrity are fundamental, as first gifts of the Creator, as is the right to religious freedom within which we express and develop our relationship with the Creator.

Human sexuality is a strong and vital component of our humanity and of our personalities. The exercise of that sexuality, in sexual relations, is something that touches the deepest aspect of our identity and personhood. A fundamental aspect of Catholic teaching about sex is that sexual acts must always take place within the context of authentic freedom. This is because, properly understood, human sexuality has the capacity to unite two people, body and spirit, at the deepest level, in a completeness of self-giving that has within it the call to a permanent commitment between them and which, of its nature, is open towards the creation of new human life. This makes clear that there is no place in sexual relations for domination, aggression, instrumentalization or any kind of dehumanization of the person. Any such behaviour is deeply destructive of our humanity.

The violation of a person's bodily integrity through sexual violence and abuse is a most fundamental denial of human dignity and a most gross offence against a person's human rights. It is an offence against the Creator and cries to heaven for judgement.

There are many forms of sexual abuse but the two I will highlight here are the sexual abuse of children and the use of sexual violence in warfare.

Sexual violence in warfare

Sexual violence as an instrument of warfare and conflict is, to borrow a phrase of Pope Francis', a deep wound in the body of humanity. That it is as old as humanity itself is a cause for our lasting shame. According to a report by the House of Lords, it has:

> for far too long been regarded as just one of those things that occurs when there is conflict. It is not; it is a war crime, which must not, under any circumstances, be overlooked or condoned. Like genocide, slavery, torture and piracy, it must be eradicated . . . [It] ruins lives, destroys families, breaks up communities and prevents societies from achieving sustainable peace.[1]

Unicef has reported that sexual violation of women erodes the fabric of a community in a way that few weapons can. The damage can be devastating because of the strong communal reaction to the violation. The pain is inflicted on entire families. When a woman is raped her whole family and culture are attacked because in many societies women are viewed as repositories of a community's cultural and spiritual values.[2]

The full horror of sexual violence defies description because of the radical and permanent damage done to the very essence, the personal sense of being, of its victims. It also defies description because of the sheer numbers of its victims and the unbelievable spread of this evil in so many parts of our world. This horror defies description because it is not the random act of men who have, for a while, lost all sense of decency, but a deliberate and ordered tactic of oppression, domination and destruction. It is to humanity's shame that the systematic use of sexual violation is still, in some places, considered as a duty of soldiers, an order that they must carry out.

A more radical burden is that the stigma attached to sexual violation falls on the victim and not on the perpetrator. What terrible collusion is indicated by that fact? This public acceptance inverts the principles of human decency and thereby reinforces so many other daily forms of oppression and disregard for the moral standards which flow from mutual respect and the rights of the person.

A crucial starting point for the struggle against sexual violence is the recognition that every human activity is subject to moral principles and judgement. If this principle is put to one side, then not only do human actions

> *Every human activity is subject to moral principles and judgement*

lose their truly human character but they risk sinking into the realms of the amoral. This principle applies to situations of warfare and conflict. No declaration of war – legitimate or not – excuses those who fight from the demands and observance of this fundamental principle of our behaviour: to preserve our humanity there are moral norms we must observe. Reflecting on behaviour in war, Catholic teaching states: 'Actions deliberately contrary to the law of nations and to its universal principles are crimes, as are the orders that command such actions. Blind obedience does not suffice to excuse those who carry them out.'[3]

In other words, war is no excuse. The demands of justice remain in place. A crime is a crime, whether or not it is committed in the context of war. And sexual violence is always a crime; it is always an immoral act.

The Church wholeheartedly backs every initiative to prevent sexual violence being perpetrated against anyone, anywhere and under any circumstances. I am proud to be able to point to the significant work carried out by many religiously motivated people in the fight against sexual violence in warfare. I salute especially the work of religious sisters, in many countries, who for decades have dedicated themselves to this work, without seeking reward or praise. They do so as part of their commitment to justice in our world today. And we are richer for their efforts, along with the efforts of many others, too. This enterprising work generates the kind of wealth without which our world cannot survive.

When I hear the testimony of victims of sexual violence and activists who work tirelessly to support victims, it is often their faith, above all else, that has strengthened them. I can state with confidence that in this struggle faith is not a problem to be solved but a powerful resource to be discovered.

Sexual abuse of children and other vulnerable people

The work of safeguarding children is a huge challenge to the Church and to society generally. Much has been learned but we must listen carefully to the survivors of abuse to ensure that the Church continues to learn and remain vigilant. There is still a great deal to do in terms of both prevention and response to this crime.

Many sectors of society throughout the world have yet to learn about the reality of abuse, about the hidden ways of these destructive offences, about the measures needed to create safe environments and about how the suffering and needs of the survivors has to shape the responses which they receive.

Yet this is particularly and sharply applicable to the Church. We must be clear as to why this is so, as to why the Church is constantly in the headlights and the headlines when it comes to this terrible feature of our world.

The abuse of children, young people or vulnerable people of any age is essentially a betrayal of trust

The abuse of children, young people or vulnerable people of any age is essentially a betrayal of trust: the abuser must first establish trust and then abuse it. This is why, as far as we know, children are less frequently abused by a stranger. When abuse takes place within the family the bonds of trust are a fact of nature and betraying that trust is a betrayal of our shared human nature. Abuse by a well-known public person, a TV star or entertainer, is the betrayal of a public trust. Abuse by a respected adult in the community – a teacher, a youth group leader or a priest – is a betrayal by the very people who should have our children's best interests at heart; it is a betrayal of the trust that whole communities place in our leaders.

Abuse within the Church, however, is also a betrayal of the trust of faith. And this is what makes it so particularly terrible for the abused person because it not only destroys her or his ability to trust in general, it also destroys her or his trust in faith. The mission of the Church is to offer and witness to the trustworthiness of the Word of God. Abuse shatters trust in God. Any form of abuse, and particularly of children, within the Church is therefore a betrayal of the very essence of the purpose and character of the Church. It is a most profound wound. When we protect and safeguard children we also safeguard the purpose and character of the Church itself.

But protecting the character of the Church must not be our focus. At the heart of all our work, and central to every policy and programme, must be preventing further abuse and helping the survivors of abuse. It is those who have been so deeply injured that must be the primary focus and motivation of this work. They have been injured in their humanity, in their capacity to trust, to relate to others and to form trusting relationships. And this is a radical wound, since we are social beings who find identity, growth, hope and joy in and through our relationships. Survivors of abuse have also been injured in their capacity for faith in God and since we are by nature spiritual beings this too is a radical injury.

We know how important the life of faith can be in enabling us, as wounded people, to find life, mercy, forgiveness, hope and joy in the Lord. This is the work of our salvation. It is the work of divine grace. To damage a person both in their nature and in their capacity to receive divine grace is to leave them profoundly burdened in the greatest quests of their life. The well-being of the survivors of abuse, and our responsibility for what has been done, must drive us forward in the work of listening to them. It is this attentive listening that enables us to respond more adequately to their needs and to create environments in which they are truly safe and feel supported.

Answers are not easy to find, but this is our challenge. We must learn more, not only about the nature and consequences of abuse, but also about how to apply high standards of safeguarding across all dioceses, religious orders and institutions around the world.

Pope Francis has consistently led the efforts of the Church to recognize the terrible consequences of this crime; to make clear that there is no place for secrecy which contributes to the damage inflicted on the victims and survivors of abuse. His leadership helps us to tackle this grave problem that exists in our community and in our entire human family. We must follow his example.

I pray that God will bless and lead us, in all humility, to tackle the evil of sexual abuse in our world, to listen and learn from our past failures, and to give comfort and help to his little ones, of whatever age, who have been wounded and, for so long, left abandoned.

For reflection or discussion

1 What do you consider the most fundamental human rights to be?
2 How does the Church support these rights?

3 What policies does your parish have in place to safeguard children and vulnerable people? How robust are they? Do they need to be reviewed and updated?

4 What can you, or your parish, do to support victims of sexual abuse and violence?

5

Ending human trafficking and slavery

Pope Francis has described human trafficking as 'an open wound on the body of contemporary society, a scourge upon the body of Christ'.[1] His words marked the inauguration of the Santa Marta Group, an alliance of international police chiefs and bishops from around the world working together with civil society to fight against slavery.

Slavery disfigures our society and calls for an unremitting effort to bring it to an end

Just as it was in the eighteenth century, human slavery is a hugely profitable 'trade'. Two hundred years after it was abolished by law, it is still one of the most lucrative crimes in the world, perpetrated by large, international criminal networks. Slavery disfigures our society and calls for an unremitting effort to bring it to an end.

An evil crying out to heaven

Christian opposition to slavery springs from a radical commitment to the dignity of every human person. Human dignity has to be protected and promoted in every circumstance and time. That dignity does not depend on the abilities or status of a person but is rooted entirely in the inner depth of the person's existence. It springs from the gift of human life that comes from the divine Creator who is the Father of us all.

Human trafficking and slavery strip people of this fundamental dignity, reducing each person to the status of a commodity. It is an evil crying out to heaven. That there are over 20 million people callously held in slavery in our world today is a mark of deep shame on the face of our human family. Words alone cannot remove it. The challenge before us is to work to our utmost to rescue, protect, assist and serve the poorest of the Father's children who are reduced and oppressed in this way.

There are three key moments in my life that have convinced me of this.

The first happened some years ago, when I listened for the first time to the witness of a young woman who had been betrayed into the slavery of enforced prostitution. Her story was heart-wrenching. But what added a particular depth to my shock was the fact that she was a young English woman, trafficked from England into slavery in Italy.

The second moment occurred at about the same time. I had begun to witness a remarkable partnership developing in London between religious women and the London police force. This partnership transformed the effectiveness of operations to rescue victims of slavery, care for them and bring to justice the perpetrators of this horrendous crime.

I realized then the effectiveness of this collaboration between such unlikely partners. The sisters involved in this work did not instinctively trust the law enforcement agencies with whom they worked. They understood, with good reason, that these agencies were likely to prosecute the very women the sisters were trying to protect. Yet over time a fruitful partnership was established. It resulted from the hard work of building trust – a work made up of many demanding practical steps, requiring changes in mindsets and procedures. For one thing, it was essential that the police were able to assure the sisters that the victims of trafficking would not be prosecuted, but rather helped to escape and to rebuild their lives.

The Santa Marta Group

The third moment was when, in 2014, at the end of the first Santa Marta conference in Rome, Pope Francis turned to me and asked me to keep this work going. That was an order that could not be refused!

Since then Santa Marta has had three further international gatherings, with law enforcement agencies from over 30 countries, and some progress has been made. For example, in Nigeria there have been efforts to tackle the root causes of human trafficking by developing the creative use of land; closer to home, a North Atlantic Maritime initiative is emerging to tackle the problems of unjust working conditions in the fishing industry; other initiatives involving the Catholic community have emerged in Argentina and Lithuania, and requests for support have come in from the Philippines, South Africa and Mozambique.

The new United Nations Sustainable Development Goals express the official commitment of every member state to work for the eradication of human trafficking and modern slavery. This goal cannot be achieved without international cooperation at many levels, one of which is to be found in the work of the Santa Marta Group, which is open to all who wish to take part in its mission.

Such international partnerships require not only a shared motivation but also some clear key aims. For us, these aims are: first, the safety and well-being of every victim of human trafficking; second, the enhancement of the work of law enforcement, including the breaking up of criminal networks and the arrest and prosecution of the perpetra-tors; and, third, the strengthening of the legal frameworks within which this work is carried out.

Whenever a short silence fell, the faces of the women were suddenly full of the inner pain and sense of loss that is in their hearts

Bakhita House

I have been fortunate to see the dif-ference that working against human trafficking can make. I was invited for dinner with eight women staying at Bakhita House, in London. This home was opened in 2015 and provides women escaping human trafficking with safety and support to allow them to begin the process of recovery. It was a wonderful occasion, consisting of a delicious, international meal cooked by the women themselves and full of laughter and smiles. However, whenever a short silence fell, the faces of the women were suddenly full of the inner pain and sense of loss that is in their hearts.

These same guests had spoken at a different time about their experience of being victims of human trafficking and of their welcome in Bakhita House. They said:

> We lost touch with our souls. We had nowhere to turn. We had nowhere to go. At one point we thought it would be the end for us. We had no hope to hold on to. We thought we would break. We did not know our strength until we came to Bakhita House. We got through our pain, with the help of the most loving and dedicated staff and volunteers. They have helped us to survive. Our faith was revived and it kept us alive.[2]

I quote these words because they are at the heart of what we are trying to achieve: not just the rescuing of the victims of trafficking, but the building of trust so that they can reassemble their lives and live again. This is a great work in the face of a dreadful evil.

The house is named after a Catholic woman, Josephine Bakhita, now the patron saint of modern-day slaves. Josephine was herself a slave: in 1877 at the age of nine she was snatched from her family in the Sudan. She spent the next eleven years in slavery, during which she was bought and sold five times and treated with the utmost cruelty. By the time she won her freedom, she had over 114 patterns of deep scars in her flesh.

Josephine had been born into a pagan family but she eventually became a Christian and joined a religious order of Catholic nuns. For 45 years she lived that life with joy and in dedicated service of the poor. Often she suffered flashbacks to her time of torture, but she died in peace and true hope in 1947. Her feast day, 8 February, is observed around the world as a day of prayer for victims of human trafficking.

Actions, not words

For me, as for many, Pope Francis remains a central and inspiring figure in this work. He is direct and blunt in what he expects of us. He expects far more than words: he expects effective action on the ground, which frees prisoners, comforts the victims, promotes their well-being and generates new hope in a world in which there is far too much suffering and despair.

In a speech to the United Nations, Pope Francis talked about the importance of 'putting an end as quickly as possible to the phenomenon of social and economic exclusion, with its baneful consequences: human trafficking . . . [and] slave labour'. He called on us to create institutions that are 'truly effective in the struggle against these scourges'.[3] He asked us to remember always that we are responding to real men and women, sons and daughters of our one Eternal Father, who are therefore truly our brothers and sisters. In their plight we are complicit. In their freedom we will rejoice with a joy no other satisfaction can give.

For reflection or discussion

1 How could you, or your parish, draw attention to the issues of human trafficking and slavery? Could you hold a special event to mark the feast day of Josephine Bakhita (8 February)?

2 Do you know how to recognize victims of human trafficking and slavery in your own community and how to report it? You could look at <http://www.ilo.org/wcmsp5/groups/public/@ed_norm/@declaration/documents/publication/wcms_105023.pdf> to find help with this.

3 What could you do to put words into actions and join the fight against modern-day slavery?

6

Hope for prisoners

In 2016, Pope Francis told a group of prisoners in Philadelphia that 'confinement is not the same thing as exclusion.'[1] With these words he reminds us that prisoners are never to be forgotten or written off. Rather, meeting the needs of prisoners is an important part of any civilized society. As Dostoevsky wrote: 'The degree of civilisation in a society can be judged by entering its prisons.'[2]

We think of ourselves as a civilized society, yet we know that in practice our treatment of prisoners often falls short of acceptable standards. If society is to make prudent use of all its resources, both human and material, it must meet the varied needs of prisoners, while insisting that they face the consequences of their criminal actions.

We think of ourselves as a civilized society, yet we know that in practice our treatment of prisoners often falls short of acceptable standards

The Church has a vital part to play in this work, not only because we wish to contribute wholeheartedly to the well-being of society, but also because, through the eyes of faith, we have a particular perspective on those who are in prison. We have a clear mandate from our Lord and

Master that we should care for them. Jesus said, 'I was ... in prison and you came to see me' (Matthew 25.36), thereby identifying himself with those behind bars.

During Advent a few years ago I was celebrating Mass in HMP Feltham. The small chapel was packed full with young men and prison staff. Our reader that day, who was serving a sentence for drug offences, spoke beautifully and with conviction. I was inspired to find that he entered prison struggling to read and write, but had been working hard with volunteers and chaplains to improve his literacy. Those efforts paid off and being chosen to read at Mass clearly meant a great deal; his sense of achievement and newfound self-confidence were strikingly visible to everyone gathered there.

Those skills also meant he had a better chance of getting a job after being released, which was due to happen in the new year. It was truly a time of hope and promise for that young man. But this hope and promise were never realized. I learnt that, within months of walking out of the prison gates, he was drawn back into the gang he had left. Shortly afterwards he was stabbed to death in a pointless feud.

This tragedy underscored for me that, despite the efforts of all those working in our prisons and the difference that can be made in many cases, the challenges to be confronted are many and complex. For as long as any prisoner finishing her or his sentence returns to a life of gangs, crime, homelessness, addiction, unemployment, violence or alienation, our society is failing and our prisons are not working as they should.

Failings in the prison system

In 2004 the Bishops' Conference of England and Wales published a report entitled *A Place of Redemption*. It expressed our vision for a system where time in prison is well used, rather than being a process of warehousing people at best and, at worst, inflicting further damage on them. More than a decade later, it feels that the realization of this aspiration may be further away than ever.

The consequences of this failure reach far beyond the lives of prisoners themselves. In particular, we must always keep in mind the well-being of every victim of crime and clearly state that shortcomings in rehabilitation result in reoffending with more innocent people damaged by further crime.

One of the most painfully clear failings in our system is the growing number of prisoners coming to harm while in prison, self-inflicted or otherwise. We all strive for a day when every prisoner walks out of the gates as a reformed individual. Yet each year more people walk out bearing new physical and emotional scars. And far too many never walk back out at all.

The figures for 2015–16 are shocking: 100 suicides; over 32,000 incidents of self-harm; over 20,000 assaults and 6 apparent murders.[3] But mere numbers do not convey the human cost, the pain, the damage, or the grieving behind them. Every one of these incidents is a tragedy. Each one is a measure of a failure by society to care adequately for those we imprison.

People in prison have done wrong. In many cases they have caused great suffering. Yet they still have the same basic dignity as every other man, woman or child. Tackling this crisis of harm within prisons must be a priority: better mental health support and safer staffing levels are not desirable additions but urgent necessities.

Building a good prison system that will help people to turn their lives around must go far deeper than addressing crucial matters of safety. It must involve courageous reforms and a genuine shift in how we view individuals who have committed crimes. It is important to remember that around a quarter of our 85,000 prisoners will have been in care as a child, at least one in three will have a mental or physical disability and half will have the literacy levels of an 11-year-old.[4]

Depriving someone of their liberty is a legitimate punishment. Throughout England and Wales there are examples of well-run prisons which are clean and tidy, where people are treated with respect, receiving the care and support they need to change their lives. However, it is a stain on our society that in the twenty-first century some prisons are still characterized by rubbish, damp, dirt, graffiti and unhygienic facilities. They are unacceptable. Nick Hardwick, the former Chief Inspector of Prisons, has highlighted how prisoners often have no choice but to eat meals in their cell right next to an unscreened toilet.[5] There is surely no justification for treating our brothers and sisters with such disregard. Worse still, by locking people in squalor we send the most blatantly negative message to society about their worth. A society which shows such contempt for a prisoner's dignity truly undermines that prisoner's chance of reforming her or his life.

Much of the outstanding work carried out in prisons is undermined by chronic overcrowding and understaffing, which means that people can be locked up for almost the entire day. It is nothing short of a tragedy how frequently prisoners are deprived of the opportunities to get a good education and to learn skills simply because there is no one available to unlock their cell door and walk them down the corridor to a classroom or workshop.

How can educational programmes or restorative justice schemes succeed when people cannot get into the study or meeting room in the first place? Sometimes cells are not opened for the basic human needs. How can we tolerate a regime where people, given just one hour out of their cell, have to choose between exercising, taking a shower or making a phone call to a relative?

Prisoners and their families

Too often family relationships are further damaged when a loved one is imprisoned far away from the family home

There is also much more that needs to be done when it comes to protecting and enabling the relationships between prisoners and their families. It is no secret that family belonging is one of the biggest incentives for people to turn their lives around. We know that prisoners who stay in regular contact with their family during their sentence are far less likely to reoffend after their release. Despite the work of organizations such as the Prison Advice and Care Trust (Pact), which supports prisoners' relationships with their families, far too often family relationships are further damaged when a loved one is imprisoned far away from the family home, thereby decreasing the chance of a reformed life.

Some prisons have been truly innovative by providing facilities to help sustain family ties. Audio-visual technology is used so that prisoners can have face-to-face conversations with family members. What a difference that must make when it comes to moments like saying goodnight to their children! Families also now have the opportunity to book visits online and prisoners can receive emails. But in other areas the benefits of technology are woefully lacking; for example, families wishing to send money to a prisoner must still fill out a postal order and pay the associated costs.

Pope Francis described the importance and the experience of family members visiting prisons:

> They undergo the humiliation of being searched. They don't disown their sons or husbands, even though they have made mistakes; they go and visit them. This seemingly small gesture is great in the eyes of God. It is a gesture of mercy, despite the errors that their dear ones have committed.[6]

Despite the tireless work of many in the prison service to facilitate contact, families who desperately want to make these visits are often prevented from doing so by the great distances that prisoners are held from their homes. For a large number of mothers with young children in particular, the cost and practicalities of travelling hours by public transport for each visit present an enormous and sometimes insurmountable obstacle. This lack of family contact serves only to deny prisoners an important help in reconstructing their lives.

Any decisions about where to locate new prisons must take into account how vital strong family relationships are for rehabilitation: prisoners must be accessible to their families.

Government reforms

Our society is failing prisoners and prisons are failing our society. We need, more than ever before, a bold and serious programme of prison reform. I was hugely encouraged when in February 2016 David Cameron announced that 'we need a prison system that doesn't see prisoners as simply liabilities to be managed, but instead as potential assets to be harnessed'.[7]

This was a long overdue acknowledgement and it opens the way for real change.

Since then, Dame Sally Coates has carried out a ground-breaking review of education in prison. Modernizing prisons, improving education and tackling violence are still on the Government's agenda.[8]

Prison reform is often misconstrued and rarely popular. It is not about being soft on prisoners or crime. It is about being civilized. It is about recognizing just punishment, reducing reoffending, genuinely helping victims and getting people's lives back on track so that they are a benefit not a burden to our communities. It is about creating a criminal justice system that delivers real justice. As Pope Francis reminds us:

> where there is mercy, justice is more just, and it fulfils its true essence. This does not mean that we should throw open the doors of the prisons and let those who have

committed serious crimes loose. It means that we have to help those who have fallen to get back up.[9]

Individual responsibility

When pursuing the cause of rehabilitation of prisoners we must never lose sight of each person's own responsibility. Even the most civilized treatment and best opportunities will come to nothing if those who have been found guilty are not themselves prepared to accept punishment, make amends and work towards a better future.

> *When pursuing the cause of rehabilitation of prisoners we must never lose sight of each person's own responsibility*

Our vision is one in which prisoners are helped to change. But prisoners must play their part. While the state has an inherent duty to care for those it imprisons and facilitate their rehabilitation, we must always insist that every person is the agent of her or his own life and accountable for her or his own actions, even though that accountability may be limited by conditions and ability.

Many chaplains undertake restorative justice work with prisoners, for example by running a Sycamore Tree course. Prisoners on the course explore the effects of crime on victims, offenders and the community, and discuss what it would mean to take responsibility for their personal actions. This is just one compelling example of how prisoners can be encouraged to come to terms with their offence and the impact of their choices on others. Such work is an integral part of any worthwhile prison system and, crucially, it benefits victims as well as offenders.

Equally, when people are released from prison, they have the responsibility to continue on a new path. Prison should equip them with the skills to do this, but hard work and commitment must come from the person.

Community responsibility

A further part of this puzzle is, of course, the role of communities, and attitudes in our society as a whole. When people who have left prison are stigmatized and rejected, is it any wonder that they return to the gangs and drug dens of their past? When people are continually punished despite having served their sentence, can we really be surprised if they sense that they have no stake in society?

Our parishes are particularly well placed to welcome people and help them get back on their feet. We must actively reach out a hand of friendship and offer practical assistance to those leaving prison. For even the smallest actions can give someone hope and help them to stay on the right path.

One young prisoner, preparing for baptism, gestured to the knife scars and tattoos on his face and neck and poignantly asked his chaplain, 'How can I walk through the door of a church looking like this?' His words are a challenge to each of us: could we confidently say to him, and others like him, 'Yes, you are welcome in our parish'?

Out of the 85,000 people in our prisons there are only a tiny minority who will never be released. Everyone else is going to re-enter our communities and live alongside us. It is in our best interests that we support them, not segregate them. Without this welcome, any redemption they found in prison and any motivation they have to reform will be wasted, along with all that they have to offer.

This will not always be easy, particularly when we are called to show compassion to those who have committed violent or serious crimes. But at such times we can draw strength from the words of Pope Francis when he tells us that 'their fall could have been mine'.[10] In different circumstances many of us might well have been led to make the terrible choices that led our brothers and sisters to prison.

True rehabilitation means not defining people by their worst action for the rest of their life. Some of the steps that we need to take are as basic as changing our use of language. Why, for example, should someone for ever be labelled an ex-offender even after they have paid their debt to society?

> *True rehabilitation means not defining people by their worst action for the rest of their life*

Ban the box

We know that for people leaving prison one of the most important aspects of rebuilding their life is finding stable employment. But for at least two years after their release they must disclose their sentence on initial application forms for employment. Every day people are instantly written off just because they have ticked that box.

I know of one man who, during his sentence for a serious crime, achieved several qualifications including a postgraduate degree. Upon release he was determined to use his skills for the benefit of others. Yet three years on and despite many applications he had not had a single interview.

It is hard to envisage the crushing disappointment of someone who has worked hard to move away from crime and learn new skills, only to be rejected for job after job and never even given the opportunity to explain how he or she has changed since being convicted years before. That is not just devastating for the individual; it deprives employers of potentially excellent and able workers and denies society working taxpayers.

This is why a growing number of socially responsible companies and public bodies are banning the box, and allowing people to disclose and discuss their conviction later in the recruitment process. Then they have a chance to put their past in context and show who they really are. Of course convictions have to be disclosed and where necessary DBS checks undertaken. But people are not simply written off without a hearing for actions in the past which may no longer have a bearing on their future.

The Church should also work towards banning the box in our own employment practices, while taking all the necessary steps to ensure that safeguarding is never compromised. All employers should be encouraged to take this step and give people a fair opportunity that will benefit our society.

On the frontline of reform

There is a long and rich Christian tradition of advocating criminal justice reform. Women and men from all Christian denominations, and from other faiths, have worked to make our system more civilized, humane and therefore more effective. Putting the gospel message into action, they have played a role in ending the death penalty, overturning unjust laws and putting the rights and needs of prisoners on the political agenda. Now more than ever we need to harness that tradition, with a strong voice and clear message.

The Church's legitimate place in the prison reform movement derives from the fact that we are not merely concerned observers, but in so many ways we are on the frontline. Chaplains are working day in, day out, in every prison across the country. Christian charities are helping thousands of prisoners and their families as well as providing vital support to people after their release. Hundreds of volunteers are visiting, teaching and mentoring people on both sides of the gates. And of course Christians can be found among the many excellent staff of the prison service.

This work is immeasurably valuable in its own right. But it also means that as a Church we have the experience and expertise actively to promote change and to work with those around us to achieve it. Indeed Pope Francis has challenged us all to re-energize our commitment to all whose lives are touched by prison. Responsibility for reform falls upon individuals, government, businesses and communities. So let us continue to help offenders be accountable for their actions, push those in power to implement bold agendas, encourage employers to play their part, and ensure that our society treats this challenge with the importance it deserves.

For reflection or discussion

1 What can your parish do to reach out to ex-offenders in the community and make them feel welcome in your church?

2 What can your parish do to help families in your community who have someone in prison?

3 What can you do to fulfil your Christian duty to bring God's mercy to those in prison?
4 How might you support the work of charities that help prisoners, such as the Prison Advice and Care Trust (Pact) <www.prisonadvice.org.uk>?

7

Resisting religious extremism

The rise in extremism, particularly among young people, is a cause of concern for us all. Just how easily extremism can take hold has been made clear to me through conversations with two people, both of whom have direct experience of the recruitment by so-called Islamic State of young people in this country. From their different perspectives, one in the context of a charity and the other in formal work on behalf of the Government, both had a similar story to tell. It was a very sobering narrative.

Both spoke about the use made of social media in the recruitment of young people to terrorism. Both spoke of the vulnerability of youngsters today as being a key factor in the influence brought to bear on them. Both were astonished at the speed at which recruits were brought 'on board'. One said that it was clearly possible to bring a person to the point of being willing to leave all for the sake of their newfound cause, even to the point of embracing violence or suicide, within a four- or five-week period.

But what was most chilling was the view that the key age for contacting and influencing these potential recruits was 14 to 15 years old. One girl that I heard about lived in

West London and was a keen member of her local sports club and captain of the girls' football team. She was on the point of travelling to Syria and was dissuaded only by the leader of the charity, after long periods speaking with her about what she wanted in life and what she stood to lose.

In one of my conversations, a phrase used to describe such youngsters was this: they are 'clean skins'. In other words no one has yet made a lasting impression on them; they are, in the classic phrase, still a *tabula rasa*, or a 'blank slate' as yet unformed by substantive values. This is a somewhat incomplete description because of course no one reaches the age of 14 without being influenced in many ways. But many do reach that age without a firm basis of values or beliefs by which they can steer their lives or against which they can rebel. In schools many have been presented only with fleeting guidance, couched always in the tones of choice: you must decide what you think is right or wrong for you; you must choose your identity. They have also been exposed to many different competing pressures and patterns of behaviour, some of which are readily seen to be shallow, others instinctively distasteful, yet demanding an adherence through social pressures.

It is to teenagers such as these that the call of a definitive, demanding faith, one which asks for a heroic sacrifice, is addressed. It is cast as a true fulfilment of all the unfocused yearning within them. One month is all it takes to transform a dissatisfied and disorientated teenager into a terrorist.

How do we define extremism?

We need to be careful in our use of language and of the word 'extremist'

It is vital that we encourage values in young people that will help them to resist the lure of extremist views and extremist actions. But we need to be careful in our use of language and of the word 'extremist'. We need a sound definition or else we could engender further alienation.

What exactly are the 'socially unacceptable' patterns of thought and behaviour that might be thought to come under the umbrella of extremism? How do we begin to define what can reasonably be seen as inimical to the society we wish to shape and protect? Is it all religious belief, as some imagine? Does it include religious convictions that, at this time, do not accord with contemporary culture and preoccupations?

My own inclination is to view actions and values as 'unacceptable' if they clearly and unreasonably impede the development of professional and personal competences fit for our economy and professional standards, such as the denial of education on the basis of gender or ethnicity; or if they contradict the shared, fundamental principles that emerge from reflection on the dignity of every person as both an individual and a social being, such as female genital mutilation with all its terrible personal and indeed social consequences; or if they undermine the call for a just society in which the dignity of each is recognized and the balance of needs and resources is constantly scrutinized and challenged, such as employment that excludes the recognition of the rights of labour, as in domestic or sexual slavery; or, finally, if they refuse to recognize, or deny an openness to, the spiritual dimension of the human person and the respect for religious freedom, in both public and private, that is its consequence.

These are quite complex criteria and there will always be points of divergence and discussion about where a balance is to be struck. But better this way than pursuing simplistic, popular criteria of acceptability that would smuggle in a 'loyalty' test along with all its potentially damaging consequences.

Social media and extremism

Social media plays a crucial part in the process of radicalization and recruitment to extremist causes. It has been proposed that there are five powerful drivers fuelling the digital phenomenon. They are: the desire to connect and be connected; the desire to access information, to know, and at speed; the desire for guidance, to have someone or some cause to 'follow'; the desire to share thoughts, convictions, expressions; and the desire to be 'entertained' or at least amused.

The digital world, in other words, caters for people who sense their isolation, their detachment from each other; who have a sense that the speed of developments is leaving them behind; who are at something of a loss as to where to turn for guidance or direction and are ready to attach themselves to something or someone who comes across with 'credibility', even if it is the credibility of celebrity or notoriety; who want very much, in their thoughts and responses, to be part of something greater; and who, on the whole, may be finding life to be rather flat, functional and boring. The potential of the digital world to respond to this experiential mix is astonishing. So too is its potential to exploit that need.

The internet has an amazing capacity to contain and convey countless pieces of information and evocative images. These fragments range over every facet of human experience and emotion. Some are glimpses of violence, of sadism, of rampant greed, of deliberate exploitation. Some depict self-loathing and a searing anger that lashes out at all. At the other end of the spectrum, there are numerous stories of heroism, of a generosity towards others that refuses to count the cost. There we meet people of astonishing humanity and of creative genius. So many things are announced in the digital world.

But the real power of this virtual world is the ways in which it can be used to assemble many of these fragments into a coherent, or at least seemingly coherent, whole and focus them into a narrative which compels and captivates. This skill can obviously be put to good use, but it is also the skill of the recruiters of violence.

Images propagated by Islamic extremist groups can quickly go viral and offer the 'certainty' and 'truth' that some vulnerable young people crave. For example, the dreadful images of Jihadi John, dressed in black, pointing upward with the bared blade of his knife, his other hand holding his victim in a position of total subservience, defeated, beaten and about to die, are prime examples of extremist propaganda.

It is proclamation – or an annunciation – to the world of what is to come, of what is held to be the truth, of how we are expected to respond. It claims to reveal the fundamental subservience of the human person to the absolute authority of the one in whose name this killing is about to take place. It announces where we are to look for our hope and how we are to behave if we are to inherit that hope. It is an announcement that everything else, everything that stands against this project or offends against this 'truth' is to be destroyed. It announces that history itself is to be purified by the shedding of blood and by the destruction of everything not inspired by this radical vision of humanity. And it claims the name of God.

We need to offer young people a different image to rally around. Contrast Jihadi John's 'annunciation' with a more classical image with some visual similarities. The figure stands upright in white, a powerful yet welcoming figure, reassuring in the face of vulnerability. One hand is held high above the head, with a finger pointing upwards, indicating the source of all that is being conveyed. The other hand of this figure stretches downwards, to the second figure, a beautiful young woman. The hand reaches out in order to raise her up in praise and thanks. The second figure kneels, not in subservience but in awe. She too has a bowed head, showing her naked neck, emanating not fear but peace, a loving readiness to say 'yes'.

The visual similarities between the two images are of course superficial. The second image, of the annunciation to Mary, announces the dignity of the human person who has been given life as an act of love and who is being invited to raise both eyes and intellect to understand the full meaning of that gift: a life to be lived in relationship, partnership with God. Here there is no threat, no defiance, no hint of destruction to come, but exactly the opposite: there is a hint of glory lying ahead.

Each of these images assembles the fragments of our lives and constructs a vision of purpose and meaning.

Each conveys energy, a depth of commitment that challenges the viewer. Each is an invitation to step forward and to find meaning, purpose, belonging and a future. One is dark, drenched in a terror which is both appalling and compelling. The other is bathed in light and offers an entirely different path, one which demands our courage and distinctiveness and which promises cooperation with the divine in the work of peace and justice.

A shared humanity

We are left with the question, how can we strengthen our young people so that they are able to resist the lure of extremist propaganda? The answer must lie in education, not in its narrowest sense of formal academic achievement but in its broadest sense of educating the whole person. It is through education that a society shapes its future.

Every person needs the opportunity to develop their potential and to see it contributing to the effort of society as it strives for prosperity. Every person benefits when she or he sees what is truly distinctive about our shared humanity, about the call of the heart, of the pathway of beauty, of creativity and diversity. Every person, and every society, needs constantly to grasp the challenges of poverty and wealth, of right and wrong, of the distinction between law and morality, the challenge of living justly.

The most profound core of the person, the true source of their dignity and rights, lies in the transcendent nature of their being

Today we hear much about 'British values', variously expressed. Essentially they are those of democracy, the rule of law, tolerance and 'equality'. At the heart of these values lies an interrelated set of ideas: that we must strive to achieve our best, in service of society; that we must awaken an innate understanding of human nature and its dignity so that we act accordingly towards our neighbours, no matter our differences; that we understand that a sense of justice and fair play are part of our character and that laws are best fashioned in true and searching dialogue and not government diktat or favour; and that we know that the most profound core of the person, the true source of their dignity and rights, lies in the transcendent nature of their being. For everyone is a spiritual being, living not simply within the contingent horizons of sovereignty, science and space but within those of eternity.

To be passionate about such values is to serve all that is best in Britain and in every society. The religious beliefs that inspire these values, properly understood and lived, are the best way to promote a deeper awareness of our shared humanity, and the best defence against those who distort and abuse their religion for violent ends.

For reflection or discussion

1 What can you and your parish do to encourage inter-faith dialogue and cooperation?
2 Is your own use of social media in accordance with your faith? Would you ever type or post something that you would not say to someone's face?
3 How does your Christian faith inspire the values by which you live, and by which you can help promote understanding, moderation and peace in the world?

Epilogue:
What makes us human?

When I was visiting a refugee centre for thousands of Christians in Erbil, the capital of Iraqi Kurdistan, I met a woman whose story left an indelible impression on me. She told me of her family's frightening and rapid flight from their home in the city of Mosul as so-called Islamic State terrorists advanced. She said that her Muslim neighbours of many, many years had wept to see them leave.

Here, in the midst of the most awful suffering, was a true sign of what makes us human. We weep.

As human beings we know, at the deepest level, what is truly good for us, and it is not the latest car or mobile phone

The tears of true weeping are powerful in all that they can express. They flow because we are heartbroken at what is or has been lost or destroyed. As human beings we know, at the deepest level, what is truly good for us, and it is not the latest car or mobile phone. Perhaps we shed a tear over them occasionally. But we do not weep! We weep at the death or departure of a loved one. We weep at wanton destruction of friendship, even at the destruction of our much loved environment. We weep because, in fact, we are not indifferent to goodness. We care passionately about all that is good, and not just about 'my personal goodness' but for all that is truly good, objectively good, good for others, for our common good.

Sometimes we weep with rage. These tears are born of our innate sense of justice, when we see a situation which is 'crying out to heaven for justice'. Often those tears will be fuelled by our sense of helplessness, for the evil being done is beyond our influence. But that does not dull our sense of outrage at innocent suffering, at horrendous abuse of a person's integrity or dignity.

Such tears come from the heart, from our inner self, from our soul. They point to that dimension of being human which goes beyond the immediate, which sees beyond the facts, to an awareness of the deeper values. They mark us out from the animal world with its refined instincts but absence of moral sense and decision-making.

There is another source of tears which we must not hide away. Each of us is capable of shedding tears of regret and of repentance. Here, perhaps, we come to the most inner part of ourselves. We reflect on our own behaviour. We judge our own behaviour. We face the uncomfortable truth of our own waywardness and we repent. This is the realm of conscience, that inner capacity within every human being, by which we recognize in what we do the difference between good and evil.

Tears of confession, when shed in the embrace of love, evoke mercy, forgiveness and hope

These tears of repentance are the most valuable. Through them we set out on the road of forgiveness, the road of new possibilities, the road of renewed freedom to start again, the road of hope. Tears of confession, when shed in the embrace of love, evoke mercy, forgiveness and hope. That is certainly true of the love of God. And when we seek and find forgiveness we, as human beings, appear in all our nobility and most powerfully reflect the image and likeness of God in which we have been created.

Then, of course, come the tears of joy. They begin in sheer relief that a burden has been laid down, a locked door sprung open. But then they become tears of wondrous gratitude that we are loved and that life again is filled with light.

Long may we weep, for then we will discover again our humanity. However, we must not look at the problems that face the world – the homeless on our streets, the victims of sexual violence, people who find themselves enslaved or lured into lives of crime – shed a tear, wipe it away and carry on with our lives. No, our tears must move us to act in ways that will help to heal these wounds in the body of humanity.

We must strive to bring God's hope and mercy to the world. For this is our calling, our God-given mission.

Acknowledgements

1 Rumours of hope

An address given at the Royal Society for the encouragement of Arts, Manufactures and Commerce (RSA), 17 June 2015, entitled 'Where do we find the generative capacities for hope?'

2 Missionary disciples

Based on an address given at the National Evangelisation Conference, Proclaim '15, in Birmingham, on the Feast of St Benedict, 11 July 2015.

3 Agents of mercy

Based on an address given at Proclaim Westminster, at the Royal Horticultural Halls, Westminster, 14 November 2015.

4 Ending sexual violence and abuse

Based on an address given at the Inter-Faith Consultation Conference at Lancaster House, 9 February 2015, and on an address (delivered on behalf of the Cardinal by Bishop Marcus Stock) to the delegates at the Anglophone Safeguarding Conference, 20–23 June 2016, in Vatican City, Rome.

5 Ending human trafficking and slavery

Based on addresses given at the Special Conference held at the United Nations on 7 April 2016 on the combating of human trafficking and modern slavery, given at the service to commemorate the work of William Wilberforce and to launch the office of the Independent Anti-Slavery Commissioner at Westminster Abbey, 12 October 2016, given at the Santa Marta Group Conference in Rome, 26 and 27 October 2016, and given on 'Pause for Thought', Radio 2, 7 February 2017.

6 Hope for prisoners

Based on an address given at the Conference of Prison Chaplains at St Mary's University, Twickenham, 6 September 2016.

7 Resisting religious extremism

Based on addresses given at: the CATSC/CES Secondary Leaders' Conference, London, 28 January 2016; the Benedict XVI Memorial Lecture 2016, Archbishop's House, 8 March 2016; the Religion, Identity and Conflict Conference at St Mary's University, Twickenham, 2 December 2016; and at the Mass offered for the victims of the attacks on Westminster Bridge and Parliament, at Westminster Cathedral, 26 March 2017.

Epilogue: What makes us human?

Based on a reflection given as part of BBC Radio 2's *What Makes Us Human* series, 1 July 2015.

Notes

1 Rumours of hope

1 Thomas Aquinas, *Summa Theologica*, Part II-II.

2 Missionary disciples

1 *Evangelii Gaudium*, 119–21.
2 Cf. International Theological Commission, '*Sensus fidei* in the life of the Church', 2014, nn. 49, 62.
3 Mother's Prayers of the Solace Community.
4 *Evangelii Gaudium*, 1.
5 Apostolic Journey of His Holiness Pope Francis to Ecuador, Bolivia and Paraguay (5–13 July 2015). Holy Mass for the Evangelization of Peoples, Homily of the Holy Father, Parque Bicentenario, Quito, Ecuador, 7 July 2015.

3 Agents of mercy

1 <www.crisis.org.uk/pages/homeless-def-numbers.html> (accessed 30 March 2017).
2 Report by Depaul UK, *Danger Zones and Stepping Stones*, 2016: <www.uk.depaulcharity.org/danger-zones-and-stepping-stones>.
3 Pope John Paul II, Homily at Krakow-Lagiewniki, 17 August 2002.
4 Sandra Schneiders IHM, *The Resurrection: Did it really happen and why does it matter?* (Los Angeles, CA, Marymount Institute Press, 2013).

4 Ending sexual violence and abuse

1 Select Committee on Sexual Violence in Conflict, *Sexual Violence in Conflict: A War Crime* (London, House of Lords, 2016).
2 *The State of the World's Children 1996*, Unicef: <www.unicef.org/sowc96/>.
3 *The Catechism of the Catholic Church*, 2313.

5 Ending human trafficking and slavery

1 Address of Pope Francis to participants in the International Conference on Combating Human Trafficking, 'Casina Pio IV', Lecture Hall of the Pontifical Academy of Sciences, 10 April 2014.
2 Sources are unnamed for legal/security reasons.
3 Address of the Holy Father at the United Nations Headquarters, New York, 25 September 2015.

6 Hope for prisoners

1 <www.catholicnewsagency.com/news/confinement-is-not-exclusion-pope-francis-visits-with-philly-inmates-28605/> (accessed 30 March 2017).
2 F. Dostoevsky, *The House of the Dead*, trans. Constance Garnett (New York, Dover, 2004).
3 *HM Chief Inspector of Prisons annual report: 2015 to 2016*: <www.gov.uk/government/publications/hm-chief-inspector -of-prisons-annual-report-2015-to-2016>.
4 *RSA Journal: Matters of Conviction*, Issue 2, 2016.
5 *The Guardian*, 29 January 2016.
6 Pope Francis, *The Name of God is Mercy* (London, Bluebird, 2016).
7 <www.gov.uk/government/speeches/prison-reform-prime-ministers-speech> (accessed 31 March 2017).
8 *The Guardian*, 19 July 2016.
9 Pope Francis, *The Name of God is Mercy*.
10 Pope Francis, *The Name of God is Mercy*.